The Four Gifts of Christmas

Advent Readings for December

by Beth Vice

Thanks be to God for His
indescribable gift!
/ Cor. 9:15
Beth
Vice

*Dedicated to my church family
at Tillamook Nazarene Church.
Thank you for being my friends, my forever family, and
supporters, cheering me on in the work God has
given me to do.
I love the way you live as Christ
in our community
and touch lives around the world.*

WHAT IS ADVENT?

When my husband and I were dating, my sister started calling Friday "Kelly Day," because I eagerly awaited his arrival each week. We met on e-harmony and communicated via email for a while, sharing our hearts. Then came the nightly phone calls. Finally, we decided we were ready to meet in person. After that first meeting, we only missed seeing each other one weekend out of our eight months of courtship.

We lived an hour and a half apart. So Kelly drove over every Friday after work. We spent that evening, Saturdays, and Sundays together, then we would part for the work week. After a few expensive hotel bills, he decided to bring over his fifth wheel and rent a monthly space at the RV park near my home.

This is what it means to anticipate the arrival of someone you love and long for. That is what we celebrate at Advent, which means "Coming."

The season begins each year on the fourth Sunday before Christmas – somewhere between November 27 and December 3. Advent gives us time to clear our cluttered minds, think about our Beloved Lord, and make room for Jesus' arrival. When He comes, on Christmas Day, we can celebrate with joyful gratitude and abandon. Much like the joy Kelly and I celebrated on our wedding day.

During Advent, like lovers daydream about their beloved, we consider what He means to us and the miracle of how we first met Him – when God came in the form of a man to show us His love. He invited us to get to know Him; He courted us, with the intension of marriage.

As a man, Jesus took our sins on himself and died on the cross as the only perfect sacrifice for our sin. Most importantly, three days later, Jesus triumphed over death and hell when He rose from the dead. Now, He reigns at the right hand of God.

And we who love Him, anticipate the *Second* Advent of Christ - when Jesus will return for His Bride, in power and glory. On that Day, He will take us to our forever home in heaven. All who have accepted the forgiveness and new life Jesus offers look forward to this Advent with the anticipation of a Bride awaiting her Bridegroom.

THE FOUR THEMES OF ADVENT:
Each week of Advent has a specific theme, based on the events and people of that first Christmas. Candlelight is a much welcome part of Christmas in the darkest month of the year.

Many churches and families display Advent wreathes with five candles. They light one, then two, and so forth, on the four Sundays before Christmas, reading scripture to go with the topic of the day. Then on Christmas Day, they light the fifth and final candle – the Christ candle. In radiant splendor, Jesus came to shine His light into our darkened world. What better way to honor Him, than to follow His example?

The four candles represent: **Hope, Peace, Joy, and Love.** These are the four gifts of Christmas. All four are embodied in the person of Jesus Christ – He is the greatest gift we have ever been given.

I pray this year, and every year, you will experience these priceless gifts – in your relationship with God
with your family and Church
with your fellow man, and
in the deepest places of your heart.

May you experience the Hope, Peace, Joy, and Love that come from knowing Jesus. He came to rescue us from sin, legalism, despair, and give us life everlasting.

To introduce the theme for each week, I chose to focus on those individuals who took part in Jesus' coming that first Christmas. I hope you savor each day of this delightful season, as you look forward to *this* year's Advent, and eagerly anticipate *the one to come.*

Merry Christmas!
Beth Vice

The Four Gifts of Christmas

HOPE

The Four Gifts of Christmas

WEEK ONE - HOPE: Simeon and Anna

Livescience.com gives a few tongue in cheek facts on wilderness survival: "If you're ever stuck out in the wilderness, remember what survival experts call 'the Rule of Threes'. You can live 3 minutes without air, though we don't recommend trying. In a harsh environment…you have 3 hours to survive without shelter. After 3 days, you need water or you'll perish. You can make it 3 weeks without food, though we promise you that won't be fun."

Though that may be true, none of us can survive for *any* length of time without hope. Hope gives us the *will* to live. This hope provides strength to endure beyond mere physical circumstances.

Simeon and Anna epitomize the unrelenting hope it takes to survive when there's no outward evidence the answer is on its way. The Israelites had long hoped their Messiah would come and save His people. Isaiah foretold His coming: "Therefore the Lord himself will give you a sign: The virgin will conceive and give birth to a son, and will call him Immanuel" which means "God with us" (Isaiah 7:14). Yet, seven hundred years had passed, and still, they waited.

Of all those still hoping, only Simeon and Anna *recognized* their Messiah at first glance. He made a surprising public appearance, as the baby of a poor couple, bringing their son for circumcision. There were no angels or heavenly phenomena, yet they knew Him instantly. Simeon and Anna had walked with God for many years, in eager anticipation. God rewarded their faith with sight.

As we enter the season of Advent, we can anticipate Jesus' coming with this same attitude of hope - however He speaks and in whatever situation He chooses to show himself to us. Like these two devoted lovers of God, I pray we will recognize our need for His deliverance and healing, and watch daily for Christ to appear.

Thank God for sending Jesus, at just the right time. He continues to be "God with us" every day of the year. This is the hope of Christmas - this is the promised One! Jesus came to bring redemption for all who will recognize and welcome Him.

Day One: It's the Same Every Christmas

We read about the same people every year. However, every Christmas, God has something new to show us from their examples. Jesus came gift-wrapped in swaddling clothes. The only ones who knew His true identity were a brave young couple, some smelly shepherds, a resentful king, a few misguided priests, and foreign stargazers. Yet heaven rang with praise and the earth rejoiced in God's plan.

Where do you find yourself in the story?

Joseph and Mary - The Weary Travelers: Luke 2:1-7
Are you traveling for Christmas this year? Is it by choice?

_____

_____

_____

How might it have been difficult for Mary and Joseph to trust God in this inconvenient trip, just before Mary's due date?

_____

_____

_____

The Innkeeper – The Harried Host: Luke 2:6-7
Have you unwittingly left Christ out in the cold this Christmas because your life is too full? What needs to change?

_____

_____

_____

How would the story have a different ending if the innkeeper had known who was in his stable that night?

_____

_____

_____

The Angelic Host - The Pageant: Luke 2:8-14

What was the purpose of their display: to draw a crowd, show off their costumes, wave at their moms?

_____

_____

_____

What was their message?

_____

_____

_____

How can we model our Christmas programs after theirs?

_____

_____

_____

The Shepherds – The Partygoers: Luke 2:15-20

These men didn't hesitate to accept the party invitation – they didn't shower, stop to buy a hostess gift, or get a babysitter for the sheep. They just went! How did it change their lives?

_____

_____

_____

How should this change our attitudes about the Christmas parties we host or attend?

_____

_____

_____

Herod - The Greedy: Matthew 2:1-3, 7-8 and 16-18

King Herod was the Grinch who tried to steal Christmas. Why?

_____

_____

_____

How does Satan try to steal Jesus' throne today?

_____

_____

_____

The Priests - The Party Poopers: Matthew 2:4-6

The priests knew the Messiah was to be born in Bethlehem, and that the Wise Men were on their way to worship Him. Yet, instead of welcoming the Messiah, they joined Herod's plot to kill Him. Why?

_____

_____

_____

What excuses do people give today for not taking time to worship Christ at Christmas?

_____

_____

_____

The Wise Men - Lavish Givers: Matthew 2:1-2, 9-12

These were not your normal baby shower gifts, but they were *perfect* for King Jesus. Gold identified His royalty, Frankincense His priestly role, and Myrrh foretold His sacrificial death.

What gift can you give Jesus this year to acknowledge His identity as your King, Priest, and Savior? What attitude or behavior needs to change to honor Him the way He deserves?

_____

_____

_____

Day Two: Shining Ever Brighter

*The path of the righteous is like the first gleam of dawn,
shining ever brighter till the full light of day.
Proverbs 4:18*

I love greeting the day when the house is quiet. I fix myself a cup of coffee and snuggle down in my comfy chair to begin the day with God.

However, it's dark when I get up during the winter months. Darkness isn't a friendly invitation to crawl from my warm bed. But I'm not ready to turn on bright lights first thing in the morning either.

That's when it's nice to have the soft light of a lamp. It shines warmth and light into the gloom of early morning, without shocking your senses. As the sun comes up, the greater light gradually fills the room drawing me into the day.

That's our job as Christians; we are lamps shining in the darkness. The world's not ready to face the glory of God in a sudden burst of light. They would be blinded, terrified, like Daniel and John were in their visions of God, described in the books of Daniel and Revelation in the Bible.

God is described as being "resplendent with light" in Psalm 76:4. That's why He uses little lamps like us to get others ready to meet Him. Our small light leads the way to His radiance.

We are the first gleam of dawn –inviting people to see more of God, drawing them into His brighter presence. As we grow in our own relationship with God, He shines more and more of His light through us.

Isaiah 60:1-3 says:
"Arise, shine, for your light has come, and the glory of the LORD rises upon you...See, darkness covers the earth and thick darkness is over the peoples, but the LORD rises upon you and his glory appears over you. Nations will come to your light, and kings to the brightness of your dawn."

Our light is nothing compared to His, but He chooses to shine through us anyway. We don't know how much time we have left to make Him known. In heaven there won't be any more darkness; God will be all the light we need. Night will never again obscure His brightness.

Until then, we need to plug in to our Source of light every day. Church attendance, Bible knowledge, and personal charm won't make us shine; only God's Spirit in us will do that. He illuminates us from within to shine on those around us searching for His hope and life to escape the darkness.

Revised excerpt from *Peace Within Your Borders,* WinePress, 1999.

Day Three: Jesus Still Believes In Me

All of us have let Jesus down. We feel we've gone too far, said too much, or not enough. We're afraid to even ask Him to forgive us...again.

People express it in various ways:
"God could never forgive me for what I've done."
"I've messed things up too much."
"It's too late."
"I'm too old to change."
"God doesn't want a sinner like me."

We're convinced the ways we've denied the Lord in word and deed have eradicated all possibility of a relationship with Him. He wants nothing to do with us. Or so we think.

Peter had a valid reason to feel he'd committed the unforgivable sin. He'd followed Jesus for three years - watched Him heal, even raise people from the dead! He saw how Jesus loved and forgave. He knew Jesus was living, breathing, truth and grace. In fact, Peter had personally declared Jesus to be the Son of the living God. Yet he denied he even *knew* Jesus—hours after swearing he would die to protect Him!

How could he ever come back now?

But Jesus still believed in him. He communicated this hope and acceptance to Peter three times –before Peter failed Him, at the moment of denial, and afterwards, to draw him back.

Before the rooster crowed Jesus said: "I have prayed for you, Simon, that your faith may not fail. And *when* you have turned back, strengthen your brothers" (Luke 22:31-34, author's emphasis).

Jesus gave Peter hope at the *moment* of betrayal. "The Lord turned and looked straight at Peter. Then Peter remembered the word the Lord had spoken to him: 'Before the rooster crows today, you will disown me three times'" (Luke 22:61-62). Some say Jesus looked at Peter to chastise him. I believe He looked at Peter with the utmost love—and hope.

Finally, Jesus showed Peter He believed in him *after* He rose again. He told Mary to tell the disciples "and Peter" that He had risen. When He met the boys on the beach with breakfast, Jesus pulled Peter aside to re-commission him for spreading the Good News of forgiveness (John 21).
Peter is the only one who received this kind of special attention. I think it's because he *needed* to know that Jesus still believed in him.

We have all failed Jesus, just like Peter, and He wants to bring us back into His fellowship. He came to earth to give us hope; He reigns in heaven now and gives us the same three assurances:

He goes **before** us. He knows the temptations coming our way and prays for us (Rom. 8:34).
He sees us the **moment** we deny Him and looks on us with love.
He is with us **after** we blow it, to forgive and equip us, to go out and tell others the Good News—God forgives anyone who will come to Him, and ask.

When Peter was filled with the Holy Spirit, he was transformed from an obstinate, loud-mouthed fisherman, into an eloquent speaker, miracle worker, and solid rock of the church. All this, because Jesus didn't give up on him. Jesus believed in Peter; He believes in you and me. That's great news!

Day Four: All That Night

Ever get a song or jingle stuck in your head? That happens to me a lot. Often, it's an advertisement I don't even like that keeps popping into my consciousness. However, I love it when I wake up with words from a praise song playing in my head. There's no better way to welcome the day!

I have a favorite song on the *iLOVE* album by Rob Baker called, "All That Night." It's written from the viewpoint of one of the shepherds who heard the news that first Christmas.

The chorus says, "I'm still singing the song the angel sang. I'm still hearing how loud the heavens rang. I'm still seeing his glory and his light. I was a shepherd on that hillside, that night."

The angel's song was the most beautiful one the shepherd had heard in his life. It only took one performance and he couldn't get it out of his head. And he didn't want to!

Sometimes the Christmas story can get ho-hum for us. We've heard the same verses from Luke chapter two year after year. We've sung the same carols until we want to shoot "Harold the angel" or the shepherds that "washed their socks by night" (as my daughter used to say). What we need is a fresh perspective.

What was it like to be a shepherd that night when the angel made the big announcement? How would it feel to be a social outcast, and yet chosen to be the first to know the Messiah had come? They were invited to meet Him *in person*. No wonder the shepherds left the field in such a hurry! No wonder they told everybody they met what happened that night!

No doubt the shepherds relived it all over again when they got back to their campfire, as their sheep snoozed nearby. I'm sure they described the most amazing night of their lives to everyone they encountered. They, in turn, took the story wherever they went.

Every year on that night, I can picture the shepherds quoting the angel's words to friends gathered round, telling them how it felt to be the first to see The King. When Jesus began teaching, I bet they went to listen. Were they still in awe they had met Him, the night God was born in human form?

Have you ever felt like an outcast, like you don't belong? Are you far away from God and His coming? Do you wish that someone would notice the work you do as valuable - that *you* are valuable?

God sees you and has a message for you: "I bring you good news of great joy that will be for all the people...a Savior has been born to you; he is Christ the Lord" (Luke 2:10-11).

There's a little bit of shepherd in all of us. It's time to listen to the angel's song and run to meet Jesus in person. Revel in the fact that you've been *invited* to the party. You won't be able to get the song out of your head, and you won't want to. Year after year you'll be telling the story to anyone who will listen – The Messiah has come! I've met Him! And I'll never be the same.

The Four Gifts of Christmas

Day Five: He's Our Only Hope

In the movie "Star Wars" Luke Skywalker accidentally discovers Princess Leah's secret message for help. The hologram hidden in R2D2 is to someone named Obi-Wan Kenobi.

"You're our only hope," she pleads. Luke is moved by her need—her utter helplessness—and is immediately ready to do whatever it takes to rescue her. (Of course it doesn't hurt that she's young and beautiful.)

If Princess Leah's call for help was able to touch the heart of this young warrior, who didn't even know who she was, imagine how God feels when we express our desperate need for Him!

This Christmas I ask myself, *Am I desperate for a closer relationship with God?* Am I aware I'm in *extreme* need of His help? Do I know I am utterly and completely lost without Him? Is Jesus my only hope?

The Jews put their hopes in the coming Messiah to rescue Israel from the tyranny of Rome. However, Jesus came to rescue *all mankind* from the tyranny of *sin*. Do we make the same mistake today - looking only for liberation from discomfort, sickness, financial ruin, worldly oppression, or the consequences of our own sinful choices?

Throughout history believers have declared Jesus is the only hope of mankind. We desperately need the eternal hope He offers, not just a temporary fix. He didn't come looking the way people expected. He didn't kill off their enemies the way they wanted. When the crowds who followed Jesus found out He wasn't going to do things their way, many abandoned Him.

At this point Jesus asked His disciples if they were going to leave Him too. "Simon Peter said, 'Lord, to whom shall we go? You have the words of eternal life. We believe and know that you are the Holy One of God'" (John 6:69). In other words, "You're our only hope."

What about you? Has God answered your prayers in a less-than-spectacular display of power that left you disappointed? Was His answer "No" when you wanted it to be "Yes?" Kind of like getting a baby when you expected a war hero?

Have you read the Bible looking for comfort and rescue, and found He's also calling you to commitment, obedience, and self-denial? It can be hard to swallow.

But Peter had it right – where else can we go? Jesus refuses to cram His God-ness into a box of our making. Salvation is His plan and He will bring it about in the way He chooses. In His perfect way.

The question is, will we recognize Him? Will we see our real need is not for an earthly hero, but a Savior? He came to rescue us from the despair of sin, and prepare us for eternal life with Him. This world is only temporary.

What have you been seeking this Christmas? Is Jesus everything you've hoped for? Is there anyone else who can meet the deepest needs of your soul? If not, look for His entrance in the quiet, humble moments of the day. Your hope will rise as you recognize He is all you need.

The Four Gifts of Christmas

Bonus Scriptures of Hope:

There's nothing like God's Word to speak to our hungry souls. So at the end of each week's devotions, you get the chance to see what the Bible has to say about the theme of the week. The scriptures for this week are on – hope.

In the spaces provided, on your own paper, or in a group discussion, respond to each passage of scripture. Possible questions to answer are:
What does the verse mean to you?
How does it especially meet your needs right now?
How are you going to appropriate this truth in your life in this Christmas season?

Why are you downcast, O my soul? Why so disturbed within me? Put your HOPE in God, for I will yet praise him, my Savior and my God. **Psalm 42:5**

_____

_____

_____

_____

Find rest, O my soul, in God alone; my HOPE comes from him. He alone is my rock and my salvation; he is my fortress, I will not be shaken. **Psalm 62:5-6**

_____

_____

_____

You answer us with awesome deeds of righteousness, O God our Savior, the HOPE of all the ends of the earth and of the farthest seas, who formed the mountains by your power, having armed yourself with strength, who stilled the roaring of the seas, the roaring of their waves, and the turmoil of the nations. Those living far away fear your wonders; where morning dawns and evening fades you call forth songs of joy. **Psalm 65:5-8**

_____

_____

_____

_____

I rise before dawn and cry for help; I have put my HOPE in your word. **Psalm 119:147**

_____

_____

_____

_____

I wait for the LORD, my soul waits,
and in his word I put my HOPE.
My soul waits for the Lord
more than watchmen wait for the morning,
more than watchmen wait for the morning.
Psalm 130:5-6

_____

_____

_____

_____

Do any of the worthless idols of the nations bring rain? Do the skies themselves send down showers? No, it is you, O LORD our God. Therefore our HOPE is in you, for you are the one who does all this. **Jeremiah 14:22**

_____

_____

_____

_____

For everything that was written in the past was written to teach us, so that through endurance and the encouragement of the Scriptures we might have HOPE. **Romans 15:4**

_____

_____

_____

_____

May the God of HOPE fill you with all joy and peace as you trust in him, so that you may overflow with HOPE by the power of the Holy Spirit. **Romans 15:13**

_____

_____

_____

_____

We who have fled to take hold of the HOPE offered to us may be greatly encouraged.
We have this HOPE as an anchor for the soul, firm and secure. It enters the inner sanctuary behind the curtain, where Jesus, who went before us, has entered on our behalf. **Hebrews 6:18b-20**

_____

_____

_____

_____

Let us hold unswervingly to the HOPE we profess, for he who promised is faithful.
Hebrews 10:23

_____

_____

_____

_____

PEACE

The Four Gifts of Christmas

WEEK TWO - PEACE: Joseph and Mary

Interestingly enough, the two most peaceful participants in the Christmas story are the ones who had the most difficult circumstances. God knew what He was doing when He chose Mary and Joseph to parent the Son of God.

He picked a young virgin of unshakeable faith and humility. She was willing to suffer misunderstanding, rejection, and possible death for her unprecedented pregnancy. She was the world's first and only expectant virgin.

We don't know much about Joseph, but he was a man of dreams and visions, who believed what God told him and then acted on it. No matter what God required - no matter what time of day or night - Joseph protected Mary and the miraculous baby she carried.

How could they so peacefully accept all that was required of them? They withstood gossip, moving from place to place, and random visits from rag-tag shepherds and wealthy wise men.

What was their secret? I believe they knew they were a part of a bigger plan - so big that it couldn't be defeated. Their peace came from knowing that the One who promised is faithful. They were content to do their part in the most powerful drama of all time.

The Four Gifts of Christmas

Day One: Accepting Plan 'B'

I like to plan ahead and have control over my life. In the old "A Team" television show Hannibal always said, "I love it when a plan comes together." It was my favorite line. However, it's a good thing that not all my schemes "come together," because they're not as good as God's perfect plan.

Just like us, Joseph and Mary had plans, or at least dreams of what life would be like when they got married. They probably pictured a quiet existence in Nazareth with Joseph doing carpentry and Mary keeping house. The scene probably included kids, friends, and worship at the synagogue. Angelic visits, prophetic dreams, and parenting the Messiah probably didn't enter their minds.

When I was growing up and things went awry, my dad would say, "I guess we'll go with plan B." Often, the situation went on to plan C or even D. It helped me learn that fretting and flailing don't help the situation. However, I still struggle with that, just a little.

My husband constantly amazes me with his cheerful flexibility. One of his favorite sayings is: "You've got to improvise and adapt." Mary and Joseph knew how to do that. Here are a few examples:

Mary's Plan A
I'll marry Joseph soon and have his children.

We'll live respectable lives of obedience to God.

We'll live in Nazareth near family.

Mary's Plan B
I'm pregnant with the Messiah by the Holy Spirit of God!

Everyone assumes I've been unfaithful, yet I know I'm blessed.

Our baby was born in a stable.

Joseph's Plan A
Mary and I will marry and raise a family.

I'll divorce Mary quietly; I don't want to see her hurt.

We have to go to Bethlehem to pay taxes; we'll live there for a while.

Joseph's Plan B
Mary's says she's pregnant by the Holy Spirit!

An angel told me to marry her; she's having the   Messiah.

We have to move our family to Egypt; Herod's out to kill Jesus.

Every time Mary and Joseph thought they knew the plan, God threw another curve. Through it all, they followed His directions with an attitude of humble obedience.

Their continual acceptance of Plan B:
> fulfilled prophesy
> revealed Jesus as the Savior of the world
> strengthened their own faith, and
> magnified their dependence on God

They demonstrated that Plan B can be even better than Plan A, and that it really wasn't Plan B at all, but **Plan G** – *God's* Plan. The best one of all.

The Four Gifts of Christmas

Day Two: The Christmas Fear Factor

I don't think we need a special episode of the "Fear Factor" to introduce us to the terrors of the holidays. We have enough trepidation in our lives to make even the bravest contestant tremble:

> Should I eat this fruitcake not knowing what's inside?
>
> Who's brave enough to put together toys that come with no instructions?
>
> Who wants to face rabid shoppers at 3:00 am on Black Friday?
>
> Can I stand another Christmas with my family who end up either fighting, or tiptoeing around each other with frosty cordiality?

Why do so many people dread Christmas? Fear seems to be a common denominator. We fear overspending, loneliness, and congregating in the same room with estranged family. We fear taking risks, loss of love, getting old, gaining weight, hopelessness, and the unknown.

Isn't this supposed to be the season for good will? Where is "joy to the world" and "peace on earth?" Is it realistic to think we can celebrate Christmas without fear? Is it possible to celebrate Christmas when genocide, natural disasters, evil, and poverty are on every side?

Fear was around that first Christmas too. In fact, every major character of the nativity had their own set of fears and anxieties. Some gave in to them, some looked beyond them, and others left them behind. The difference was how Jesus factored in.

Fear of Rejection

Mary was troubled by the angel's opening line, yet her only question was a scientific query, "How will this be...since I am a virgin? (Luke 1:34)." Unlike anything we might have said in such a moment, Mary just wanted to know *how* God was going to do it. After He told her she went on from there with faith and bravery that boggle the mind. She must have had fears and doubt, but her words reveal only complete trust in her Lord.

She laid down her preconceived (couldn't resist the pun) ideas about what she wanted in life. She looked beyond the gossip of the moment to the place of honor she would have throughout history. And perhaps most admirably, she kept her comments to herself when most of us would have leaned into the limelight, and expressed our own opinions.

Fear of Being Unneeded

Then there's Joseph. How important did he feel as a husband and father? He wasn't Jesus' dad, or even mentioned in prophesies about the Messiah. We don't have a single quote from his lips in the Bible and he completely drops off the page after Jesus' twelfth year.

Yet, he willingly did his part - he got Mary safely to Bethlehem, delivered this God-formed baby without any training or help, moved to Egypt in the middle of the night to escape Herod, and raised Jesus as his own. If Joseph did fear insignificance, he overcame those feelings to do what had to be done, without any fanfare or complaint.

Fear of the Unknown

The shepherds were literally minding their own business, the night they received news of the Messiah. Unwelcome in social situations, and unaccustomed to polite company, they might have been afraid to arrive unannounced at the birthplace of a King. Yet, emboldened by their heavenly invitation, they ventured into unknown territory and left the stable with a story to tell.

Fear of Missing Out

The wise men, or astrologers, who came to Bethlehem looking for the new King, had one great concern. After all their effort and travel they didn't want to miss the One whose star they had followed for so long. Theologians estimate it may have taken up to *three years* before they arrived at the house where Mary and Joseph had settled. They never let fear keep them from their goal.

Fear of Giving up the Throne

Of all the characters in this story, King Herod and his followers were the *only* ones whose fears became reality.

More than anything, King Herod was afraid the prophecies would come true and he would lose his throne. He was willing to do anything to ensure the continuation of his rule - including wide-scale infanticide.

The irony is, in murdering all babies under three years of age, he not only revealed his true character, but he fulfilled *another* of prophecy about Jesus' birth:

"Then what was said through the prophet Jeremiah was fulfilled: 'A voice is heard in Ramah, weeping and great mourning, Rachel weeping for her children and refusing to be comforted, because they are no more'" Matthew 2:17-18

This further proved Jesus' identity as the promised King.

Defeating the Fear Factor

Do you experience any of the same fears these people did? How can we keep fear from ruining the heart of Christmas? Each person in Jesus' story has something to teach us about facing fear.

From Mary, we can learn to let go of our preconceived expectations regarding – gifts, decorating, family times, church programs etc.

Joseph shows us how to rejoice in being a part of God's story, even if we don't have a major role in family gatherings, gift-giving, or Christmas programs.

The shepherds are amazing examples of learning how to be less self-aware. They focused their full attention on Jesus – instead of how they looked to everyone else, and what people thought of them.

The wise men teach us diligence in our search to glimpse the face of God.

Finally, the bad guy in the story. King Herod struggled with the thing which probably troubles us the most - giving up the throne so Jesus can reign supreme. I pray we won't make the same mistake and give in to fear, but go to Him and bow in worship instead.

The Four Gifts of Christmas

Day Three: Peace With Our Appetites

So whether you eat or drink or whatever you do,
do it all for the glory of God.
1 Corinthians 10:31

I'm always impressed with people who have a healthy approach to eating. I have a history of food addiction, and even though the Lord has delivered me from bingeing, I still struggle sometimes with the role food should have in my life.

At the time the verse above was written, the Corinthian Christians struggled with whether or not God was okay with them eating meat after it had been offered to idols (Since blocks of wood and stone don't eat much).

My struggle is resisting the urge to grab a piece of chocolate every time I pass the candy dish. Or indulge in a juicy steak dinner when my clothes are already too tight. It's a question of how to practice self-discipline when there are scrumptious dishes at every holiday gathering, and church event.

Food has long been a place to bury my sorrows, my companion in times of loneliness, the guest of honor at every party, and a forbidden delight. So in a way, it boils down to the same thing. Whenever any of our appetites grow out of control they are, for us, an idol.

Perhaps this isn't an area of difficulty for you, but I suspect it is for many. Our society is obsessed with food—either super sized and mega-calorie, or fat and calorie "free." We swing from feeling pious about our high-fiber, vegan diets, or riddled with guilt about the processed sugar and flour we consume. Packaged and fast foods lighten our schedule, especially in this busy season, but add to our guilt.

So what's the answer? The real issue is not what we eat or don't eat, but our *attitude* about food and how it affects our relationship with God and others. A pious attitude smacks of Pharisee-ism; guilt is not a Christian virtue either. Both harm our witness. Both distance us from others. Neither is a heritage we want to pass on to the next generation.

Chapter ten of first Corinthians provide us with three guidelines for making peace with our appetites:
1. Eating should not be a selfish activity.
2. Our eating shouldn't cause others to stumble.
3. Our habits and attitudes about food should honor God.

Selflessness
Overeating, hoarding, and insensitive comments to others all reveal self-centeredness. Expecting others to adhere to our diet, or rejecting another's hospitality are also self-centered actions. Paul suggests thankfully eating portions of whatever is offered, without making an issue of it. I couldn't help but notice he used the word "portions."

Concern for Others' Welfare

The second guideline says, *"Do not cause anyone to stumble...not seeking my own good but the good of many"* (verses 32-33). What we say and do can encourage others to make peace with food, and appreciate their bodies as the temple of the Holy Spirit. We want to encourage *realistic* expectations of body image, in ourselves and others, not leading others into temptation or false guilt.

Desire to Honor God

The third guideline is an umbrella for *every* appetite that gets out of balance, and we have many. Everything we do should be for the glory of God and helpful to others. Hard to remember when we're eyeing that piece of pumpkin pie with our stomach already groaning after the meal. Only God can give us the answer to that dilemma, and He will, if we ask.

The Four Gifts of Christmas

Day Four: Peace With Giving

But just as you excel in everything –
in faith, in speech, in knowledge,
* in complete earnestness and in your love for us –*
see that you also excel in this grace of giving.
2 Corinthians 8:7

The cookie making day had been a huge success. The four families in our homeschool co-op made dozens of sugar cookies and valentines for widows and widowers in our churches and neighborhoods. It was time to clean up the flour and sugar, and go deliver the goods.

"Girls," I called, "it's time to get a plate and choose the cookies you want to give for Valentines."

They were less than enthusiastic - lethargic even. My youngest chose six cookies without any frosting and plunked them down on a plate. I told her those were the leftovers for us to eat. The *frosted* ones were for giving away. I got a snarly pout.

Her older sister cheerfully told me she had given away her prettiest cookies to the other kids - who had promptly eaten them. She didn't want to give away cookies someone else had decorated.

We had spent all day making goodies to bless others and my children didn't have a clue what we were doing!

Embarrassed and angry, I went into lecture mode about how important it is for us to show love to widows and widowers who might be feeling especially lonely on Valentine's Day. Red-faced and sullen, they put some cookies on a plate and we left to make deliveries.

Praise God for His tenderness when we are riddled with anger and selfishness. None of us had the right attitude, but He made it into a joyous occasion anyway. We arrived at the office of a recent widower from our church and our excitement began to mount. He didn't know it, but we had conspired with his secretary to deliver cookies to him there.

When we explained our mission, tears welled up in his eyes and he hugged each of us. He sampled a cookie, squeezed us again, and told us how much he missed his wife. He was thankful to be remembered on Valentine's Day.

He continued to pour out gratitude until we finally said goodbye. As we left, I couldn't help but ask, "Aren't you glad we didn't give him a plate of *plain* sugar cookies?"

My daughters' eyes widened and they nodded. "He needed those cookies a lot more than we did!" It was a learning experience for us all. We learned what a blessing it is to give to others, even if at first it's hard to let go of the goods.

Thinking about giving is easy – especially at Christmastime. But carrying out the plan with a cheerful spirit can sometimes be hard. Giving to people other than family and friends takes time and planning. God calls us to excel in giving whenever possible –gifts of time, money, work, tears, hugs, prayer...and cookies.

Dear Lord, help me overflow in generosity this season. Help me be willing to give away what I would rather keep, when my brothers and sisters have a need. You gave everything for my sake; teach me to be like you.

Revised excerpt from *Peace Within Your Borders*, WinePress, 1999.

Day Five: When You Get Hoicked

Change is inevitable, but it has one common denominator - very few of us like it. We've all experienced transplants of one kind or another. If not locations, we've changed jobs, or churches, or started a new relationship. Every change brings a corresponding emotional and spiritual reaction – good, bad, or most often, a mixture of the two.

I came across a delightful word in Jan Karon's Mitford series—"hoick." It means to move or abruptly transplant, to lift or pull with a jerk. That's a perfect description of how I feel about most changes - like I've been hoicked!

"He and Cynthia had been transplanted that was all. He knew from years of digging around in the dirt and moving perennials from one corner of the yard to another what transplanting was about. First came the wilt, then the gradual settling in, then the growth spurt. That simple. What had Gertrude Jekyll said to the gardener squeamish about moving a plant or bush? "Hoick it!" God had hoicked him and he'd better get over the wilt and get busy putting down roots." (from *A New Song*)

When we know God is behind the transplant, it's a little easier to accept. Even then, there's a wilt time before we begin to recover and grow again. However, it's not always God who does the hoicking.

Sometimes *others* do the hoicking for us. Sometimes *circumstances* dictate our need to move to a different place – physically, spiritually, or emotionally. And sometimes, *we* move ourselves to a new place because we feel the need for change.

Regardless of the source, and especially if the change is abrupt, we resist being uprooted from our comfortable surroundings and plunked down somewhere new. Even when we know the change is for the better.

It can be lonely at first. We may not know how to act. We might not even know why we're there.

The bottom line is, we can accept the wilt, settle in, and grow and flourish, or we can curl up and die. Those are the options.

Give thought to how many people in the Christmas story were hoicked. They had the same choices we do. How did their responses affect the outcome of their future lives, and eternal destiny?

_____

_____

Your story:
What changes have you gone through in the last year?

_____

_____

_____

_____

What stage are you currently in: the wilt, settling in, or the growth spurt? Or do you feel like part of you has died?

_____

_____

_____

_____

What healthy things are you doing to recover from the transplant so you will eventually bloom again?

_____

_____

_____

_____

What is your prayer today?

_____

_____

_____

_____

_____

_____

Bonus scriptures of Peace

In the spaces provided, on your own paper, or in a group discussion, respond to each passage of scripture on peace.

What does the verse mean to you?
How does it especially meet your needs right now?
How will you receive God's peace this Christmas season?

Numbers 6:24-26 - "The LORD bless you and keep you; the LORD make his face shine on you and be gracious to you; the LORD turn his face toward you and give you peace."

_____

_____

_____

_____

Psalm 4:8 - In peace I will lie down and sleep, for you alone, Lord, make me dwell in safety.

_____

_____

_____

_____

Psalm 29:11 - The Lord gives strength to his people; the Lord blesses his people with peace.

_____

_____

_____

_____

Proverbs 14:30 and 17:1 - A heart at peace gives life to the body, but envy rots the bones. Better a dry crust with peace and quiet than a house full of feasting, with strife.

_____

_____

_____

_____

Isaiah 9:6-7 - For to us a child is born, to us a son is given, and the government will be on his shoulders. And he will be called Wonderful Counselor, Mighty God, Everlasting Father, Prince of Peace. Of the greatness of his government and peace there will be no end.

_____

_____

_____

_____

Isaiah 26:3 - You will keep in perfect peace those whose minds are steadfast, because they trust in you.

_____

_____

_____

_____

Isaiah 32:17-18 - The fruit of that righteousness will be peace; its effect will be quietness and confidence forever. My people will live in peaceful dwelling places, in secure homes, in undisturbed places of rest.

_____

_____

_____

Isaiah 52:7 - How beautiful on the mountains are the feet of those who bring good news, who proclaim peace, who bring good tidings, who proclaim salvation, who say to Zion, "Your God reigns!"

_____

_____

_____

Isaiah 54:10 – "Though the mountains be shaken and the hills be removed, yet my unfailing love for you will not be shaken nor my covenant of peace be removed," says the Lord, who has compassion on you.

_____
_____
_____
_____

Isaiah 55:12 - You will go out in joy and be led forth in peace; the mountains and hills will burst into song before you, and all the trees of the field will clap their hands.

_____
_____
_____
_____

Luke 2:14 - "Glory to God in the highest heaven, and on earth peace to those on whom his favor rests."

_____
_____
_____

John 14:27 - Peace I leave with you; my peace I give you. I do not give to you as the world gives. Do not let your hearts be troubled and do not be afraid.

_____
_____
_____

John 16:33 - "I have told you these things, so that in me you may have peace. In this world you will have trouble. But take heart! I have overcome the world."

_____

_____

_____

_____

JOY

The Four Gifts of Christmas

WEEK THREE - JOY: The Shepherds and Angels

Joy runs exuberantly throughout the Christmas story. No one exhibits more joyous abandon regarding Jesus' arrival on earth than the shepherds and angels. Both the *givers* of the good news and those *receiving* it displayed unabashed enthusiasm.

Our Christmas pageants echo that joy. Golden-haired girls in sparkly halos sing sweetly about Jesus' birth, and smile and wave at the crowd. Shepherd boys bound down the aisle vying for first place to reach the manger, sometimes dropping staffs and stuffed sheep in the process.

Even those who are supposed to play antagonists in the show sometimes can't resist joining the good guys. Like the Innkeeper, who after saying his line, "There is no room in the Inn," suddenly blurted out, "but you can have my room!"

However, joy is much more than momentary happiness with our circumstances. It's the impossible, deep down, solid assurance that Jesus has come and He is the King. Because of that fact, all will be well. We're invited to join the shepherds and angels in celebrating the news.

Day One: Giving to Jesus

Years ago we started a tradition at our house. It helps us remember that even though we enjoy giving gifts to each other for Christmas it's really *Jesus'* birthday. On Christmas Eve we each write what we want to give Jesus in the coming year on a 3x5 card. Then we put it somewhere on the tree.

On Christmas morning, before opening stockings and gifts, we share what we've written with each other. It's my favorite part of Christmas. It opens our hearts to God and family like nothing else does.

Over the years we've given Jesus: a servant's heart, patience, not arguing back, a bolder witness, a softer tongue, the steering wheel (or throne) of our life, our careers, and many other things. After Christmas morning we each put the card in our Bible or someplace we'll see it throughout the year, and be reminded of our promise.

Like asking for wish lists from family members before I go shopping, I start asking Jesus what He wants for Christmas ahead of time as well. It makes sense to find out what people really want, rather than trying to guess. It's not much of a blessing to buy them what I want, if it's not special to them, or grab the first thing I come across in my hurry to exit the store. Why not give Jesus the same consideration?

Why not honor the "birthday Boy" with something special? Giving to God and to others is always on His "wish list," and such a central theme of Christmas. God gives us a few tips in the Bible about the kinds of giving that mean the most to Him.

Give Willingly
Each of you should give what you have decided in your heart to give, not reluctantly or under compulsion, for God loves a cheerful giver. 2 Corinthians 9:7

Give the Good News
The Spirit of the Sovereign LORD is on me, because the LORD has anointed me to proclaim good news to the poor. He has sent me to bind up the brokenhearted, to proclaim freedom for the captives and release from darkness for the prisoners, to proclaim the year of the LORD's favor and the day of vengeance of our God, to comfort all who mourn, and provide for those who grieve. Isa. 61:1-3

Give to the Needy
There will always be poor people in the land. Therefore I command you to be openhanded. Deuteronomy 15:11

Give to Please God Above Self or Others
"When you give to the needy, do not announce it with trumpets, as the hypocrites do…to be honored by others…But when you give to the needy, do not let your

left hand know what your right hand is doing, so that your giving may be in secret. Then your Father, who sees what is done in secret, will reward you." Matthew 6:2-4

Are you thinking about what you'll give Christ this Christmas? Like me, you may fail many times throughout the year to accomplish your goal perfectly. However, if your heart's desire is to give your *self* to God, He will appreciate that more than anything else.

Even if you're the only one in your household who celebrates Jesus' birthday so far, I pray your time of giving to Him will be precious and meaningful. May we joyfully say, "Merry Christmas - Happy Birthday Jesus!"

The Four Gifts of Christmas

Day Two: We're Having a Boy!

What could bring more joy than a long-awaited baby to parents, or a people, who had all but given up hope? At a time in Israel when having a boy was all-important for carrying on the family line, inheriting ancestral land, and serving in the Temple - a boy brought special joy.

In those days, people didn't have any way of knowing whether the mom was carrying a boy or girl. Unless of course a messenger from God told you ahead of time. Mary and Joseph already knew – the gender, the name to give their baby, and what His role would be in history.

In the Christmas story, we have two such birth announcements – one about John the Baptist and the other, Jesus. Look at the similarities and differences in each set of parents. Think about their responses to the heavenly messengers, and what they have to teach us about our own expectations.

The Two Announcements
Please read their birth announcements in Luke 1:5-38

What was Zechariah's situation in life?

_____

_____

_____

What was Mary's?

_____

_____

_____

How would being the father of John the Baptist change
Zechariah's   life?

_____

_____

_____

How would giving birth to the Messiah change Mary's?

_____

_____

_____

How did their responses differ when they received the
news?

_____

_____

_____

Put yourself in each ones' place. How would you have
reacted?

_____

_____

_____

The Two Mothers
Please read Luke 1:39-56
What is unusual about Mary and Elizabeth's relationship?

_____

_____

_____

What does Mary praise God for in her song?

_____

_____

_____

Elizabeth told Mary God would bless her for believing He would keep His promises (verse 45). We can claim this promise for our situations too. Personalize it by writing your name in the blanks below:

"Blessed is _____who believes the Lord will fulfill His promises to _____!"

What promise is God asking you to believe?

_____

_____

_____

The Two Births
Please read Luke 1:57-80
How has Zechariah changed over the months?

_____

_____

_____

Please read Luke 2:1-21, 39-40
What else do we learn here about Mary?

_____

_____

_____

How does Zechariah's song in Luke 1 differ from Mary's?
How are they similar?

_____

_____

_____

How was Jesus' birth different from John's?

_____

_____

_____

Two Final Questions
How did these two babies change the world?

_____

_____

_____

In what ways would like to model your life after, or avoid the pitfalls of, these two sets of parents?

_____

_____

_____

_____

_____

Day Three: In Mary's Place

You men might find it a stretch to imagine you're a young virgin who's just been told you're going to be the mother of the Messiah. But you don't have to be a woman to imagine the thoughts and feelings she might have had in her situation.

The first thing the angel said to Mary was, "Greetings, you who are highly favored! The Lord is with you" (Luke 1:28).

Do you feel like *you're* highly favored by God? Can you sense His presence in your life? You may not be as famous as Mary, or get your news from angels, but God values you just as much. The Lord sends His greetings, and wants you to know He's with you.

The next thing the angel said to Mary was, "The Holy Spirit will come upon you, and the power of the Most High will overshadow you. So the holy one to be born will be called the Son of God" (Luke 1:35).

It was a onetime event in history that a virgin would get pregnant and physically bear the Messiah. But you and I can bear the image of Christ to the world spiritually. If you have asked Jesus to be the Lord of your life, His Holy Spirit has come upon you and overshadowed you. When He did, Jesus was born anew in you. Congratulations! You are a Christ-bearer!

How did Mary respond to all this? Did she freak out, push the angel out the door, and lock it behind him screaming, "Forget it! Find somebody else!"

No, she calmly answered, "I am the Lord's servant...May it be to me as you have said" (Luke 1:38). What an amazing girl! Remember, she was a teenager – probably around thirteen years old.

She knew showing up pregnant before marriage would mean gossip, disgrace, and possible death by stoning, yet she willingly submitted to God's plan.

Can you call yourself God's servant? Are you willing to accept His plan for your life, even if others don't understand or support your decisions?

Here's where the joy comes in. Mary sings: "My soul glorifies the Lord and my spirit rejoices in God my Savior" (Luke 1:46b-47).

Does that describe how you feel? Do you lift your voice to God daily in the midst of the Christmas hubbub, to just love Him? Are you rejoicing in God your Savior from the deepest part of your being?

And there's more: "...for he has been mindful of the humble state of his servant. From now on all generations will call me blessed" (Luke 1:48). Mary described *herself* as a servant. She realized others would call her blessed - not because of anything *she* had done, but because of what *God* was doing through her. In the same way, our humble service to God will lift Him up and bring us blessings for eternity.

Mary ended her song with, "the Mighty One has done great things for me—holy is his name" (Luke 1:49). Who could call getting pregnant out of wedlock; a long, uncomfortable trip to pay exorbitant taxes; giving birth in a stable; and having to watch your child die a gruesome death on a cross (for sins He did not commit), great blessings?

Mary had spiritual eyes to see God's plan was perfect and eternal, even though it caused her momentary discomfort, and wrenching heartache in this life. Oh God, give us that same vision to wholeheartedly rejoice in your plan.

Day Four: Joy Stealers

Christmas should be the most joyous season of the year, but for too many it's more of a painful reminder of what they *don't* have – a happy family to celebrate with, a job that pays enough to provide gifts and delicious treats, a loving companion to share it with.

This is Satan's goal – to steal our joy. Instead of focusing on the joy that Jesus brings, the enemy of Christ fills our thoughts with:

Worry and envy

Unrealistic expectations regarding presents, clothes, programs, family time

Distractions – decorating, shopping, busyness, work

Physical discomfort from overeating, lack of exercise, injury, or illness

In her wonderfully transparent book, *Choose Joy*, Kay Warren shares about her own struggle with depression. Her definition of joy has helped me in my own fight with the cycle of sadness:

"Joy is the settled assurance that God is in control of all the details of my life; the quiet confidence that ultimately everything is going to be alright; and the determined choice to praise God in all things."

Joy is a choice. We choose to look beyond ourselves to see God, and trust in His character and His plan.

Every individual who welcomed Jesus modeled this quality. Zechariah and Elizabeth, Mary and Joseph, the angels and shepherds, Simeon and Anna, and the wise men – all rejoiced in Jesus. Herod and the religious leaders, who chose not to welcome Jesus, expressed no joy.

Only the angels had comfortable and perfect lives. Yet, instead of complaining about what they *didn't* have, how far they had to travel, their poor living conditions, or how long they had to wait – those who loved Jesus chose to rejoice in Him and the hope He brought.

How can we be more like them?

Follow the Star
The Wise Men looked to the heavens to find the true Star of Christmas. We find Jesus when we look for Him in the Bible every day. In this personal, timeless book, He gives us direction and comfort. If we keep seeking Him, we'll find Jesus from beginning to end - Genesis to Revelation.

Trust and Wonder
"An old Chinese philosopher was asked what was the greatest joy he had found in life. 'A child,' he said, 'going down the road singing after asking me the way.'"
~*Bulletin*, Mansfield, Ohio

At Christmas, we need to remember the wonder and joy of that first moment when we found The Way - when we realized our sin separated us from our Creator God. When we asked Jesus to forgive our sins, and show us how to live this life for Him, while on our way to heaven.

If you haven't done that yet, today is the day! Ask Him now and experience the joy of singing as you confidently walk the road of life with Him.

Let Jesus Live Through You

"Joy flows not to people who have fulfilled their desires or fallen into the right circumstances, but to people who've developed a certain kind of character – the character of Christ." ~John Ortberg

We often experience our greatest moments of joy, not when we have everything we want, but when we live freely and fully in the will of God. Jesus was a man of joy like no other, because He lived to please His Father.

How would Christmas, and life, be different if we committed ourselves freely and fully to doing the will of God?

Day Five: A Reason to Sing

They will celebrate your abundant goodness and joyfully sing of your righteousness. Psalm 145:7

In the year 200 A.D. an edict went throughout the Roman Empire that all people were to vow allegiance to Caesar as Lord. All those serving in the Imperial Army were required to worship Caesar as a god. One cohort marching across Northern Italy had forty born again believers who refused to obey the order.

"We are Christians," they explained to their captain, "and can worship no one but God."

The captain didn't know what to do with these rebels and went to his superior, a man who hated Christians and was only too glad to take the matter into his own hands. He told the men that they would renounce Christ, or face death in the Alps of the Apian Way.

That night, as temperatures dipped below zero they were stripped of their clothes and placed out on the icy glacier to "think about it." If they recanted, they could join the others at the fire, if not, they would perish. What did they do?

They began to sing.

"Forty brave soldiers for Christ," they sang, huddled together as best they could. "We are forty brave soldiers for Christ." Their voices echoed through the valley.

This went on for a while, until one man couldn't stand it any longer. He leaped to his feet and said, "Caesar is lord," and ran for the warmth and comfort of the fire.

There was a moment of grief-filled silence. Then, they began again, "Thirty-nine brave soldiers for Christ. We are thirty-nine..."

"No wait!" a voice called out. Their captain, who had witnessed their willingness to die for Christ, looked at them with tears in his eyes. With one last glance at the fire he stood up, stripped off his clothes, and went to join his men on the ice.

"*Forty* brave soldiers for Christ. We are forty brave soldiers for Christ!" he began. Their song had won his heart. He went to heaven with them that night.

***

Years later in Poland, during WWII, Maximilian Kolbe was sent to the Auschwitz concentration camp. He had been arrested for his faith along with two other priests. Despite hard work and meager rations, Maximilian often gave away his food and prayed with the discouraged.

One day an inmate escaped and the commander decided ten men would die to pay for his rebellion. Each inmate was announced by number. One man sobbed uncontrollably when they called his, "My wife, my children!"

Maximilian Kolbe stepped to the front. "Herr Kommandant, I wish to make a request, please. I want to die in place of this prisoner." The commander was speechless. Then, with a nod, he agreed.

The ten were marched to the death cell, stripped of their meager clothing, and locked inside the death hut. There, they would watch each other die of starvation. However, instead of the usual cries of terror and agony, this time there was singing in the cell. Maximilian sang every one of the others through the hours of agony, and then he breathed his last.

The joy of knowing Jesus came to earth in the form of a man, to show us the fullness of God's love, gives us a reason to sing. Our circumstances don't negate His love and sacrifice for us. May this realization empower us to face our most difficult times, as it did these brave men - with singing.

Revised excerpt from *Peace Within Your Borders*, WinePress, 1999.

The Four Gifts of Christmas

Bonus scriptures on Joy

Respond to each passage on joy:
What does the verse mean to you?
How do you especially need His joy right now?
How can you choose God's joy this Christmas?

Joy In Difficult Times
Nehemiah 8:10 - "This day is holy to our Lord. Do not grieve, for the joy of the LORD is your strength."

_____

_____

_____

_____

Hebrews 12:1-3 - Let us run with perseverance the race marked out for us, fixing our eyes on Jesus, the pioneer and perfecter of faith. For the joy set before him he endured the cross, scorning its shame, and sat down at the right hand of the throne of God. Consider him who endured such opposition from sinners, so that you will not grow weary and lose heart.

_____

_____

_____

_____

Joy in God's Presence
Psalm 16:11 - You make known to me the path of life; you will fill me with joy in your presence, with eternal pleasures at your right hand.

_____

_____

_____

_____

Psalm 28:7 - The LORD is my strength and my shield; my heart trusts in him, and he helps me. My heart leaps for joy, and with my song I praise him.

_____

_____

_____

_____

Expressing Joy in Praise
Psalm 66:1-2, 4 - Shout for joy to God, all the earth! Sing the glory of his name; make his praise glorious. All the earth bows down to you; they sing praise to you, they sing the praises of your name.

_____

_____

_____

_____

Jude 1:24-25 - To him who is able to keep you from stumbling and to present you before his glorious presence without fault and with great joy—to the only God our Savior be glory, majesty, power and authority, through Jesus Christ our Lord, before all ages, now and forevermore! Amen.

_____

_____

_____

_____

Discovering Joy in Righteousness
Proverbs 10:28 - The prospect of the righteous is joy, but the hopes of the wicked come to nothing.

_____

_____

_____

_____

Sharing His Joy
Luke 2:10-11, 17-18 - The angel said to them, "Do not be afraid. I bring you good news that will cause great joy for all the people. Today in the town of David a Savior has been born to you; he is the Messiah, the Lord"…When they had seen him, they spread the word concerning what had been told them about this child, and all who heard it were amazed at what the shepherds said to them.

John 15:11-13 - "I have told you this so that my joy may be in you and that your joy may be complete. My command is this: Love each other as I have loved you. Greater love has no one than this: to lay down one's life for one's friends."

---

1 Peter 1:8-9 - Though you have not seen him, you love him; and even though you do not see him now, you believe in him and are filled with an inexpressible and glorious joy, for you are receiving the end result of your faith, the salvation of your souls.

LOVE

The Four Gifts of Christmas

WEEK FOUR - LOVE: The Wise Men

Love gives. It can't help it. The real gift may not be a package under the tree. But be assured, where there is love, there's giving involved. It may be time, acts of service, touch, words of praise, or encouragement. These things can be given by the poorest lover. Those who love *always* find a way to give to the object of their affection.

We assume the Wise Men were kings or wealthy astrologers because of the gifts they gave. But what if they weren't? What if they spent every penny they had, risked their reputations, and left everything behind, out of love for the King of Heaven?

They traveled from the Orient to the Holy Land to find Jesus. Theologians estimate it took them three years to get there. Even if they were wealthy to start with, food and travel accommodations along the way must have cost them dearly.

Yet, they couldn't help it. The promised King of all men was going to be born in their lifetime. They were not going to miss it! They wouldn't arrive empty handed either. Would we do the same? How much do we love Jesus? How much are we willing to give to Him and to others in His name?

Day One: Don't Forget Jesus!

By now your home is probably decorated for Christmas, with lights, candles, a tree, and nativity sets of various kinds. Imagine what would happen if you forgot to put the figure of Jesus in the manger. Mary, Joseph, the shepherds, and wise men would all gaze adoringly, worshipfully…at an empty space in the crèche!

I made a similar mistake a few years ago – in public. The line I was supposed to sing in the Christmas cantata was, "Born to be Messiah; God's only begotten Son." However, at dress rehearsal I belted out, "Born to be Messiah; God's only *forgotten* Son."

Even though no one seemed to notice, I turned three shades of red. It posed an important question for me to think about, however. Have I forgotten Jesus this Christmas?

It happens. We get wrapped up in ourselves and the excitement of the season, and forget the essential gift of Christmas. An appropriate translation of Jeremiah 2:32 might say, "Do my people forget to buy presents, decorate their homes for Christmas, or eat themselves into oblivion? Yet my people have forgotten me - the *reason* for Christmas - years without number."

I began to examine my heart to see if I was forgetting Christ in the holiday excitement. My bungled lyric turned out to be a good reminder. I hope these thoughts help you remember to keep Christ in Christmas as well.

Entertainment:
Many "Holiday" movies have nothing to do with the reason for the season. They're either fluffy sentiment or blatant myths. I want to fill my mind and heart with books and movies that highlight changed lives, sacrificial giving, healed relationships, and the hope Jesus came to offer.

Schedule:
We get so busy with shopping, parties, church, and family events, not to mention practices for the Christmas cantata or baking for bazaars and potlucks. Meaningful time with the Savior can get squeezed out. Yet without Jesus, Christmas means nothing. Time with God every day is essential.

Decorating:
One night, to greet my husband after work, I lit candles everywhere and had soft Christmas music playing.

"How beautiful!" he said, "It's like entering another world." On a whim, he started counting the nativity scenes in the living room. "Hmm, are you trying to make a point here?" I laughed. The way we decorate tells the world, and us, what we're truly celebrating. I want my home to exude Jesus in every way.

Shopping:

Then there's shopping. Buying gifts for our growing family can easily take over my thoughts. It's tempting to spend months in a shopping frenzy. I have forgotten Jesus at times in all the excitement and planning for our family gift exchange. It helps to keep reminding myself why I'm giving to others. My first love needs to remain with my Savior.

Circumstances:

Christmas is often dampened by lack of finances, illness, or heartbreak. In my loneliest years, the idea of Christmas cheer stuck in my throat. But even in immobilizing pain, I realized the message of Jesus is not obliterated by our suffering. It's *enhanced*. Jesus came to love us in the *midst* of our pain, to show us a future where sin, worry, and heartache can never touch us again.

No matter how painful our circumstances, they are still temporary. Jesus—God's gift of love—meets our greatest need. He is God's only begotten Son.

Day Two: Love That Anticipates Needs

My husband and I went white water rafting a couple years ago. I was once again amazed at the way he expresses his love for me. For the third time that summer, we'd planned an outdoor adventure, expecting hot weather. Each time it was cloudy and cool.

My husband knows how easily I get cold, and how much I hate it. So, unbeknownst to me, he brought a warm, heavy sweatshirt in two layers of plastic bags, and put it in our boat. When we stopped for lunch and I was wet and miserable, Kelly wrapped me in a thick, dry sweatshirt. I was warmed by his loving anticipation of what I would need and the trouble he went to for my comfort.

This is Christmas in miniature. God knows our greatest need, our weaknesses, our pain. He knew before time began that man would sin in the Garden of Eden and had already made a plan to save us.

Before we could appreciate it, we had to realize how utterly inadequate we are to maintain sinless perfection through rule-keeping. The entire Old Testament proves what a dismal failure we make of keeping the Law. *No one* can live a sinless life, except Jesus Christ himself.

It's like my body's inability to stay warm on its own. I jokingly tell my husband I'm part reptile, because I immediately take on the temperature of my environment. I crave the rays of the sun to warm my bones.

God has given us a place in His Son. His love anticipated our need and He provided a way for us to get to heaven through Jesus. We didn't know we would need Him, but God did.

At just the right time, as we shivered in the misery of our sin, God sent Jesus to reveal His immense love, and sacrifice His life for us. He paid the debt for our rebellion that we could not. His free forgiveness warms us like nothing else can. Our walk with Him on earth prepares us for eternal life with Him in heaven.

You see, *at just the right time*, when we were still powerless, Christ died for the ungodly... But God demonstrates his own love for us in this: *While we were still sinners*, Christ died for us. Romans 5:6, 8 (emphasis mine).

Day Three: No Strings Attached

Many theologians believe the Wise Men gave their gifts, not only for their practical uses, but also as symbols of Jesus' identity – gold for His role as King; frankincense representing His priestly role for mankind; and myrrh foreshadowing the spices used to embalm Jesus' body after His death on the cross.

If that is so, it must have been hard to resist informing this young couple how important these gifts were. After all, they had been traveling for years to meet the King and wanted to greet Him with appropriate gifts. The couple must have looked young, inexperienced.

Yet, the Wise Men set down their packages of gold, frankincense, and myrrh, and resisted the urge to give Joseph and Mary instructions on how to use them.

"Now, be sure you don't fritter this gold away; it's a valuable commodity and we intend for you to use it wisely. Why don't you put it in savings? Better yet, I could keep it for you until you need the money..."

"And be careful how you use this incense and myrrh. These are valuable resins for medicinal use, not for everyday cosmetics and home fragrance. You might want to keep them for emergencies..."

These men of the Orient have much to teach us about gift-giving, especially when we're giving to Jesus. They gave with no strings attached.

It's a natural human tendency to want the person receiving our gift to value and appreciate it. However, I've heard more than once from wise men and women, that once you give a gift, it belongs to the receiver. It is up to them to decide how and when they will use it, *if* they will use it, or if they will *re-gift* it to someone else in need. Do we show Jesus this courtesy?

I know I've been guilty of offering my time, money, talents, family, body, mind, and many other things, with certain restrictions.

"I want my husband and children to serve you wholeheartedly, Lord, as long as you don't call any of them overseas to live."

"I give my work to you, Lord, and I pray you will use it for your glory...and make me successful and admired."

"Here's my body, Jesus, I give it to you. Only don't let me get sick, or injured, or have to suffer in old age, and, what's that, Lord? You want me to practice self-control in my eating, exercise, fasting, and prayer?"

The question is probably not whether we *want* to give to Jesus. Giving is an automatic outpouring for those who love Him. The question is do we *trust* Him to use our gifts in the best way possible, especially when it doesn't make sense to us at the time?

If we trust Him, we can, like the Wise Men, lay our gifts at His feet and release them into His care. Our job is to believe He will use our gifts well. Given in faith, Jesus can use even our small and insignificant offerings, to accomplish His good and perfect will.

The Four Gifts of Christmas

Day Four: The Best of Intentions Gone Awry

Have you ever made big plans to show someone how much you loved them and had it end in disaster? When my husband turned 50 I planned a surprise "Hawaii 5-0" party for him. It took months of planning – catered Hawaiian meat, invitations sent out, costumes, decorations, and music.

But two significant things happened to derail the party. I spent the night before in alternating bouts of vomiting and diarrhea. The next morning my stepdaughter was rushed to the emergency room, and had to be taken from there to a hospital an hour away, for tests and treatment.

As I pulled on my Hawaiian dress I said to him through gritted teeth, "You can't go with her to the hospital! You'll have to drive up later. I'm throwing a "surprise" party for you. I've been planning it for months and people are coming from all over. You *have* to be there!" It didn't feel like a loving plan to either of us at the time.

***

There is a similar dilemma in the classic short story, *The Gift of the Magi* by O. Henry. A poor young couple plan to buy each other a magnificent gift for Christmas. Jim wants to buy a beautiful comb set for Della's long flowing hair.

Della wants to buy Jim a chain for his prized possession – a watch inherited from his father and grandfather.

Desperate for money to make their purchases, they each sell what they most value – Della sells her long hair to buy the chain, and Jim sells his watch to buy the comb set. Of course, that renders both the gifts useless. In the end, the gift they bestow on one another is worth much more – sacrificial love. It is a Christmas to remember.

Often, our efforts to demonstrate our love for God fall through, just like the examples above. Sickness, medical emergencies, shortage of money, unforeseen circumstances etc. make it impossible to give to Jesus as we planned.

My husband told me later how sweet it was that I went to so much trouble to give him a surprise party. Jim and Della treasured the intent behind their gifts. And despite the fact that our plans often fail to live up to our aspirations - to give Jesus our best - He sees our love for Him, and that's what He wants most of all. Our hearts.

Day Five: Self-Imposed Limits

At Easter, we often talk about the sacrifice Jesus made for us on the cross. Too often we forget His sacrificial giving began long before that day. Jesus, the Son of God, chose to put limitations on himself, in order to demonstrate His great love for us.

First of all, the God of creation allowed His Spirit to become flesh in the cramped womb of a young virgin. For nine months, the physical body of God-in-the-form-of-man developed and grew.

He chose to come into a family that was not well off. He worked with His hands, in sweat and sore muscles, as a carpenter. He helped with His younger brothers and sisters – the natural children of Joseph and Mary.

He limited himself to the maturing process. From infancy to manhood, Jesus experienced all the bumps and bruises, fatigue, disappointment, stinging words, as well as every temptation we face in our humanness.

Jesus put limitations on himself in His ministry. He could have performed flashier miracles to convince everyone who doubted. He could have blasted everybody that didn't believe in Him and show who He really was. Yet, He limited His presentation in order to draw true seekers who wanted to believe.

On the cross Jesus limited himself to the full extent. The lyrics to, "It Was Love" by Abandon, say it wasn't the nails that held Jesus on the cross, but His love for us. He could have escaped the pain, humiliation, burden of our sins, and separation from His Father at any time. Yet He held back His righteous power by the *greater* power of His love. He stayed until the work was finished.

Jesus allowed His physical body to experience death. It stayed dead for three days to prove to all scoffers that His resurrection was the real deal.

In light of all He's done for us, it seems only reasonable - for those who declare we love Jesus - to be willing to limit ourselves in ways that demonstrate our love for Him. Not in legalistic rule-keeping, but as an outpouring of gratitude.

We are free to act as we wish. But true love chooses to limit its own desires for the sake of the beloved.

Am I willing to limit the way I use my mouth? To speak words that best express my love for God, and the people He has created (including myself)? To hold back words that tear down, discourage, and confuse?

Am I willing to put limits on how I fulfill sensual appetites - eating, drinking, sexual intimacy, leisure activities – because I love Jesus more than myself?

Am I willing to put limits on my most intimate relationships, choosing as my closest friends or marriage partner, those who obey Him in word and action?

Am I willing to limit the time and money I keep for myself, and give to Him first, knowing He's the One who gave it to me in the first place?

Christmas is a time of giving, but it's also time to think about limits. Do you find yourself seeking the central role in the drama of life? Would you give it up to Jesus for Christmas?

Bonus Scriptures on God's Love for Us

Respond to each passage on God's love for us.
What does the verse mean to you?
What words draw you in?
How is God calling you to respond to His love this Christmas?

His Protecting Love:
Psalm 36:7 - How priceless is your unfailing love, O God! People take refuge in the shadow of your wings.

_____

_____

_____

_____

Psalm 42:8 - By day the Lord directs his love, at night his song is with me— a prayer to the God of my life.

_____

_____

_____

_____

Love that Listens:
Psalm 66:20 - Praise be to God, who has not rejected my prayer or withheld his love from me!

_____
_____
_____
_____

Love that Gives:
John 3:16 - For God so loved the world that he gave his one and only Son, that whoever believes in him shall not perish but have eternal life.

_____
_____
_____
_____

1 John 3:1: See what great love the Father has lavished on us, that we should be called children of God! And that is what we are!

_____
_____
_____
_____

Love that Sustains:
2 Thessalonians 2:15-17 - So then, brothers and sisters, stand firm and hold fast to the teachings we passed on to you, whether by word of mouth or by letter. May our Lord Jesus Christ himself and God our Father, who loved us and by his grace gave us eternal encouragement and good hope,

encourage your hearts and strengthen you in every good deed and word.

_____

_____

_____

_____

Unconditional Love:

Titus 3:3-7 - At one time we too were foolish, disobedient, deceived and enslaved by all kinds of passions and pleasures. We lived in malice and envy, being hated and hating one another. But when the kindness and love of God our Savior appeared, he saved us, not because of righteous things we had done, but because of his mercy. He saved us through the washing of rebirth and renewal by the Holy Spirit, whom he poured out on us generously through Jesus Christ our Savior, so that, having been justified by his grace, we might become heirs having the hope of eternal life.

_____

_____

_____

_____

Our Example of Love:

1 John 4:7-12 - Dear friends, let us love one another, for love comes from God. Everyone who loves has been born of God and knows God. Whoever does not love does not know God, because God is love. This is how God showed his love among us: He sent his one and only Son into the world that we might live through him. This is love: not that we loved God, but that he loved us and sent his Son as an atoning sacrifice for our sins. Dear friends, since God so loved us, we also ought to love one another. No one has ever seen God; but if we love one another, God lives in us and his love is made complete in us.

_____

_____

_____

_____

Jude 1:1-2 - To those who have been called, who are loved in God the Father and kept for Jesus Christ: Mercy, peace and love be yours in abundance.

_____

_____

_____

_____

I pray these four gifts of Christmas, God's

hope, peace, joy, and love

will rest on you,
fill you, and
flow from you

in this delightful season, and all through the coming year.

Merry Christmas!

Look for these additional books by Beth Vice. Available on Amazon, Christian Book Distributors, or at your local bookstore:

40 Days of Lint: A Playful Twist to Prepare Your Heart for Easter

Louie the Lemon, for children 4-7, Louie finds out how to value who he is and how to respond to bullies

***Taking Back October:
For Believers in Pursuit of
Godly Fun*** instead of the
secular celebration of
Halloween

ilove Devotions
**Combining inspirational
thoughts with
contemporary music to
enrich your worship
experience**

Moments for Homeschool Moms
**A year of inspiring weekly
devotions for Home Educators
Beth Sharpton**

Photo by Tara Newman @ Selaphotography

To contact Beth Vice regarding book orders, speaking schedule, or blog, write to her at: jer3113@hotmail.com

Become a follower of her blog Epiphany at www.bethvice.blogspot.com
"Celebrating moments of discovery and growth in the daily walk of faith."

Made in the USA
San Bernardino, CA
29 September 2016